LB-ACW 004

Civil War Sketch Book 4 Illustrations by Alfred Rudolph Waud

Luca Stefano Cristini
color plates by Alfred Rudolph Waud 1828-1891

SOLDIERSHOP PUBLISHING

AUTHORS

Alfred Rudolph Waud (1828 – 1891) was an American artist and illustrator, born in London, England. He is most notable for the sketches he made as an artist correspondent during the American Civil War.

Luca Stefano Cristini has edited various publications on ancient and contemporary historical themes, including books on thirty years war, Medieval, Napoleonic as well as several illustrated books with historical color photographs. He has also curated all the brands of Soldiershop publishing. Here is the author of preface, text and captions.

Title: **Civil War sketch book 4 - Illustrations by Alfred Rudolph Waud**
By Luca S. Cristini & Anna Cristini. Plates by A.R.Waud. First edition by Soldiershop. June 2020
Cover & Art Design: Luca S. Cristini. ISBN code: 978-88-93276085
Published by Luca Cristini Editore, via Orio 35/4- 24050 Zanica (BG) ITALY. www.soldiershop.com

Alfred Rudolph Waud 1828-1891

General Winfield Scott (second from right) giving orders to his aides for the advance of the Grand Army. by Alfred R. Waud

ALFRED R. WAUD, THE ARTIST OF THE NEW YORK ILLUSTRATED NEWS

Many films have been made about the American Civil War and yet many books have been written. At the same time, the American Civil War was the first major conflict to leave behind an extensive photographic record. However, perhaps not everyone is aware of another form available to understand the feelings that those terrible years brought with them: drawings. One of the factors that make these sketches, drawn on any available material, particularly interesting is that they may be a better instrument for capturing movements, actions or emotions than the photographs of the time. In both the photographic record and the more official war art, as engaging as they can be, there does seem to be something important missing: the immediacy and intimacy of everyday life as a soldier. Unlike photographs, which shoot and immortalize a precise and unrepeatable moment, drawing is not so immediate. The artist needs time to represent what his eye is observing, and in this time the subject actually changes, he moves, he's dynamic. If one can imagine drawing a battle, it is automatic to think about the speed of the hand and the "schizophrenia" of the drawing that will result, and it is precisely this stylistic nervousness that manages to make those who have never experienced war, fortunately, understand how inglorious it can be. At the same time, we can admire drawings made in moments of calm and camaraderie between soldiers: moments of everyday life in which you can read on the faces of the characters portrayed tiredness, homesickness, scars and wounds of war... And rarely smiles. Many of the drawings that we will present later on have their respective captions written by the authors, and thanks to them we discover more details about the scene described. The authors we will consider in these volumes are three: Adolph Metzner, Edwin Forbes and Alfred Waud.

Alfred Robert Waud was born in London, England, on October 2nd of 1828. He grew up surrounded by his four siblings with a dream: becoming a marine painter. With this strong intention, he went to study at the Government School of Design, the actual Royal College of Art, and the Royal Academy of Arts, in London, and at the same time he worked as a painter of theatrical scenery. When the Hendrik Hudson ship sailed for New York in 1850, Waud decided to jump on, and pursue the job of his dreams in the United States, same thing that his brother William would do five years later. He first worked with the actor and playwright John Brougham and then found employment in a Boston periodical, The Carpet Bag, as an illustrator, providing drawings for books such as Hunter's Panoramic Guide from Niagara to Quebec. Between 1855 and 1856 he married Mary Gertrude Jewell and they went to live in Orange, New Jersey, where they raised their family. While waiting to be naturalized as an

American citizen on January 10th 1870, Alfred decided to change his middle name in Rudolph. It was in 1860 when he became a "special artist" for the New York Illustrated News and, as we have already described in the previous volumes of this series, the period during the American Civil War was a time when all images in a publication had to be hand drawn and engraved by skilled artists. That's because, although photograpghy already existed, it was impossible to transfer a photograph to a printing plate before the advent of the halftone process for printing photographs. The equipment

Chickamauga battle by A.R.Waud

was to bulky to be used on battlefields, while artist such Waud (and Forbes and Metzner) would do detailed sketches in the field, which were then rushed by courier back to the main office of the newspaper they were working for.

In April 1861 Alfred Waud was sent to cover the Army of Potomac, the main Union military contingent. Of the three artists we took in consideration in this series, Waud was the only one that covered the entire war period, for he attended every battle of the Army of the Potomac between the First Battle of Bull Run in 1861 and the Siege of Petersburg in 1865. He first illustrated General Winfield Scott in Washington, D.C., and then entered the field to render the First Battle of Bull Run in July, where both him and the photographer Matthew Brady came close to being captured by the enemy. Waud followed a Union expedition to Cape Hatteras, North Carolina the next month and witnessed the Battle of Hatteras Inlet Batteries. That autumn, he sketched army activity in the Tidewater region of Virginia. Toward the end of 1861 he went to work for the Harper's Weekly, and in 1864 his brother William, who up to that time had been working with "Frank Leslie's Illustrated Newspaper", as Edwin Forbes, joined him and they worked together during the Petersburg Campaign. Alfred was one of only two artists present at the Battle of Gettysburg, while his depiction of Pickett's Charge is thought to be the only visual account by an eyewitness.

Armed with a pencil and a sketchbook, Alfred Waud created an incomparable record of the Civil War with his lively and detailed sketches that captured all the fury and chaos of the battlefield, best rendering the idea of the schizophrenic pictorial style described in the preface. Waud's keen eye and deft pencil strokes were the means by which many Americans experienced episodes of the Civil War and visualized the cities and towns of mid-America. If Metzner's peculiarity was his ability to capture the pathos of the scene described, and Forbes' skill resided in his detailed realism and wise use of perspective, we can imagine an Alfred Waud hungry for events to be portrayed as quickly and ferociously as possible, in line with the succession of battles. After the war, he continued to contribute sketches to *Harper's*, documenting American life in locales ranging from the Reconstruction era South to the western frontier, achieving his greatest fame in his post-War work. As a freelance illustrator, he contributed work to a number of publications, including the popular, copiously illustrated *Picturesque America* (1872–74), edited by William Cullen Bryant. He died in Marietta, Georgia, in 1891.

THE PLATES

Ellsworth's Chicago Zouaves, 1861

Group of Rhode Island Soldiers. Company C 1861 ca. April-August

Camp of the second Connecticut regiment at Washington, in a grove on the north side of the city- Near New York 7th, 1861, 20 May

The 71st reg. N.Y. at Alexandria 1861, May 24-31

Surrender of the revolting Garibaldi Guards to the U.S. Cavalry 1861 June 8

Scene on the dock at the Rip Raps. Testing the Sawyer gun and projectile, a shell bursting on the rebel batteries at Sewells Point 1861 August

Flag of Truce 1861 August

Scene in the camp of the Washington Greys. 8th N.Y.S.M. 1861 April-August

The bivouac feast after a successful forage in the enemies country after the occupation of Munson's hill, 1 October 1861

Guard Mount in the Camp of the 1st Mass. Vol. Opposite the rebel position on the Potomac near Budds Ferry 1861, October 20-28

Thanksgiving in camp sketched Thursday, 28th november 1861

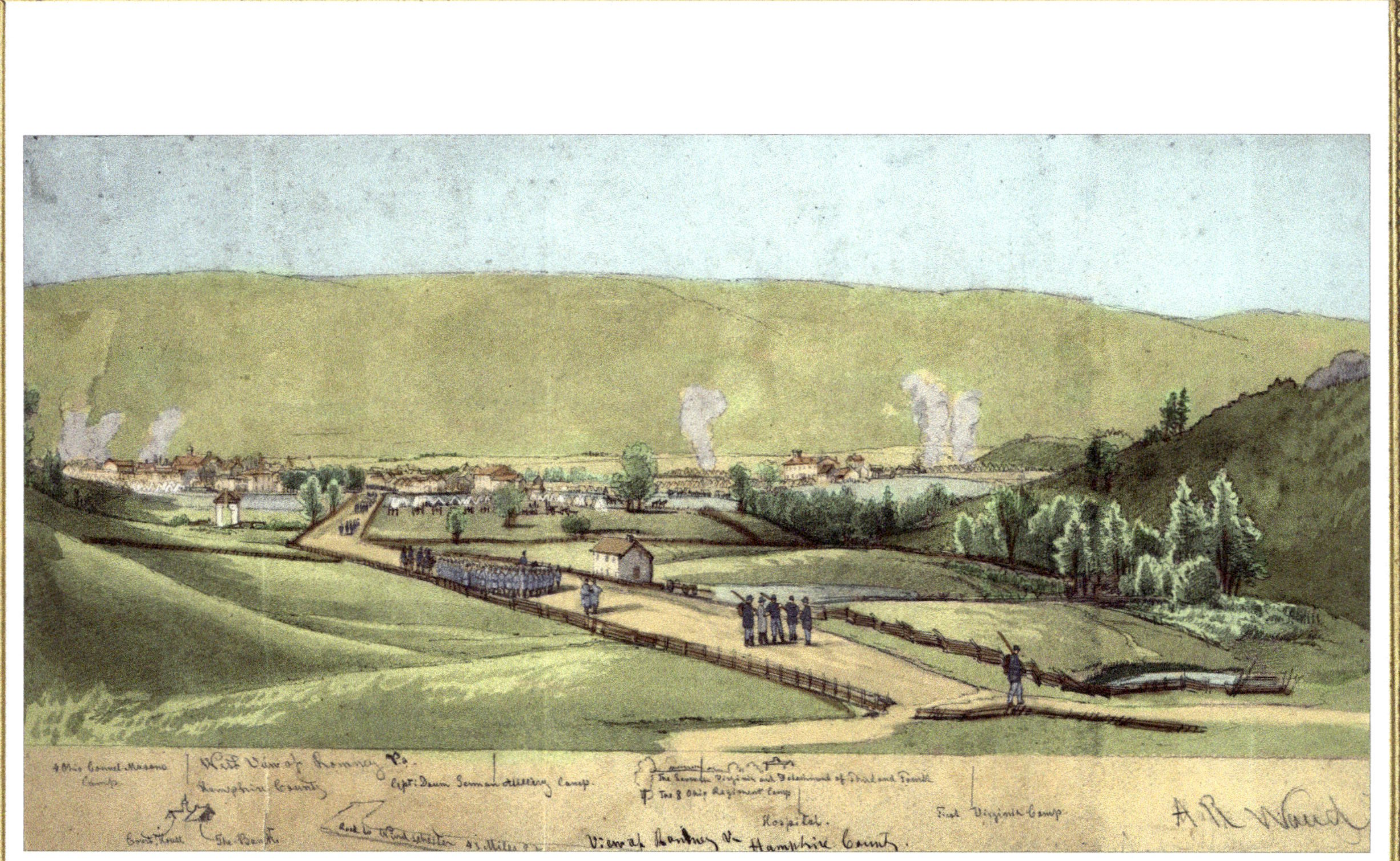

View of Romney, Va. Hampshire County between 1861 and 1862, January 10

Portion of Rebel battery at Wynns Mill. The gun which wounded Lieut. Wagner. Topographical Engineer 1862 ca. April

Pursuit of the flying rebels from Yorktown Sunday morning 1862 April-May

The Mozart (40th N.Y.) and the Scott Life Guard (38th N.Y.) taking possession of the Red Redoubt nr. Yorktown, Sunday, 6 A.M. 1862 ca. April-May

The Nelson House Yorktown used as a hospital by the rebels 1862 May

Going to the trenches a sketch in Camp Winfield Scott. Before Yorktown 1862 May

Commencement of the battle of Hanover Ct. House 1862 May 27

Guerilla warfare. Unarmed Union soldiers fired at by farmers on the James River 1862 ca. July 8

Fitz-John Porter's Headquarters 1862 July

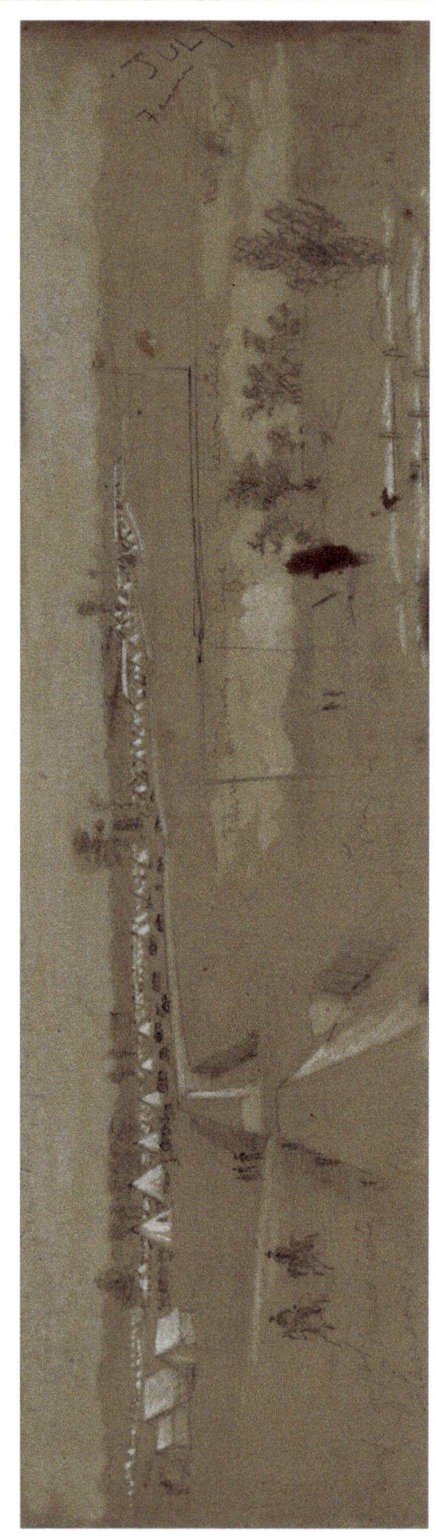

Camp of 1st Mass. Arty, Harrisons landing 1862 July

Scenes near Richmond 1862 ca. July

Street in Falmouth, Va. 1862

"Why the Army of the Potomac doesn't move 1862

Gunboats shelling the enemy at the battle of Malvern hill sketched from McClellans headquarters 1862 July

Kimmidges Creek, left defence of the camp at Harrisons Landing 1862 July-August

Middleton M.D. near South Mountain 1862 ca. September 14

The rebel dodge to cover the retreat into Virginia. Flag of truce to look after the wounded 1862 ca. September

Union soldiers exchanging salutations with the Confederates at Fredericksburg, Nov 1862

Signal Telegraph Machine and operator - Fredericksburg Dec. 1862

Building pontoon bridges at Fredericksburg Dec. 11th 1862

Catletts Station where Stuart made a raid and captured Pope's baggage 1862 December

Attack on the rebel works. Fredericksburg. Dec. 13th 1862

Skinkers Neck on the Rappahannock below Fredericksburg, VA 1862 ca. December

Pickets Near Fredericksburg 1862 ca. December

The picket guard. "Who goes there?" "Friends." "Dismount one friend, advance and give the countersign" 1863 January

Genl. J. Hooker's. Tent Hdqts. Army of Potomac 1863 ca. March

Stables and Negro servants tent, had.qtrs Army of the Potomac 1863 March

Adjutant Generals office head quarters, Army of the Potomac 1863 March

Commissary dept. Hd.qts. Army of the Potomac 1863 March

Army Mail leaving HdQts. Post Office. Army Potomac 1863 March

Marriage at the camp of the 7th N.J.V. Army of the Potomac, Va 1863 March 18

Russells Brigade, 1st div. 6th Army Corps, crossing in Pontoons to storm the enemies rifle pits on the Rappahannock 1863 April

Pontoon bridges erected for Sedgwicks corps to cross upon April 1863

Bridges built for Reynolds Corps, sketched from Rebel rifle pits 1863 April 28-30

8th Penn Cavalry, crossing at Ely's Ford, before battle of Chancellorsville 1863 April-May

Victorious Advance of Genl. Sykes (regulars) 1863 May 1st

Couch's hd.quarters and afterwards center of our line of battle 1863, May 3

Explosion of a rebel limber at the battle near Middleburg June 1863 21st

Shelling the rebel rifle pits on the Rappahannock--previous to the third crossing of Sedgwicks corps June 1863

Monocacy R.R. Bridge 1863 ca. June-July

Entrance to Gettysburg--sharpshooting from the houses 1863 July

Gettysburg. View of the hills on the left of our position from the Rebel artillery, last Rebel shot 1863 between July 1 and 3

Near the cemetery, Gettysburg retiring disabled artillery 1863 July 1-3

Hancock at Gettysburg 1863 July 1-3

Marching prisoners over the mountains to Frederick, M.D. 1863 July

Execution of five deserters in the 5th Corps 29 August 1863

The first gun at Chickamauga 1863 September 18

General Patricks punishment for gamblers 1863 October

Straggling soldiers crossing the Rappahannock above the burnt bridge October 1863

Fight at Kelly's Ford. Sleeper's battery 1863 November 7

Scene at Germanna Ford--6th Corps returning from Mine Run 1863 November-December

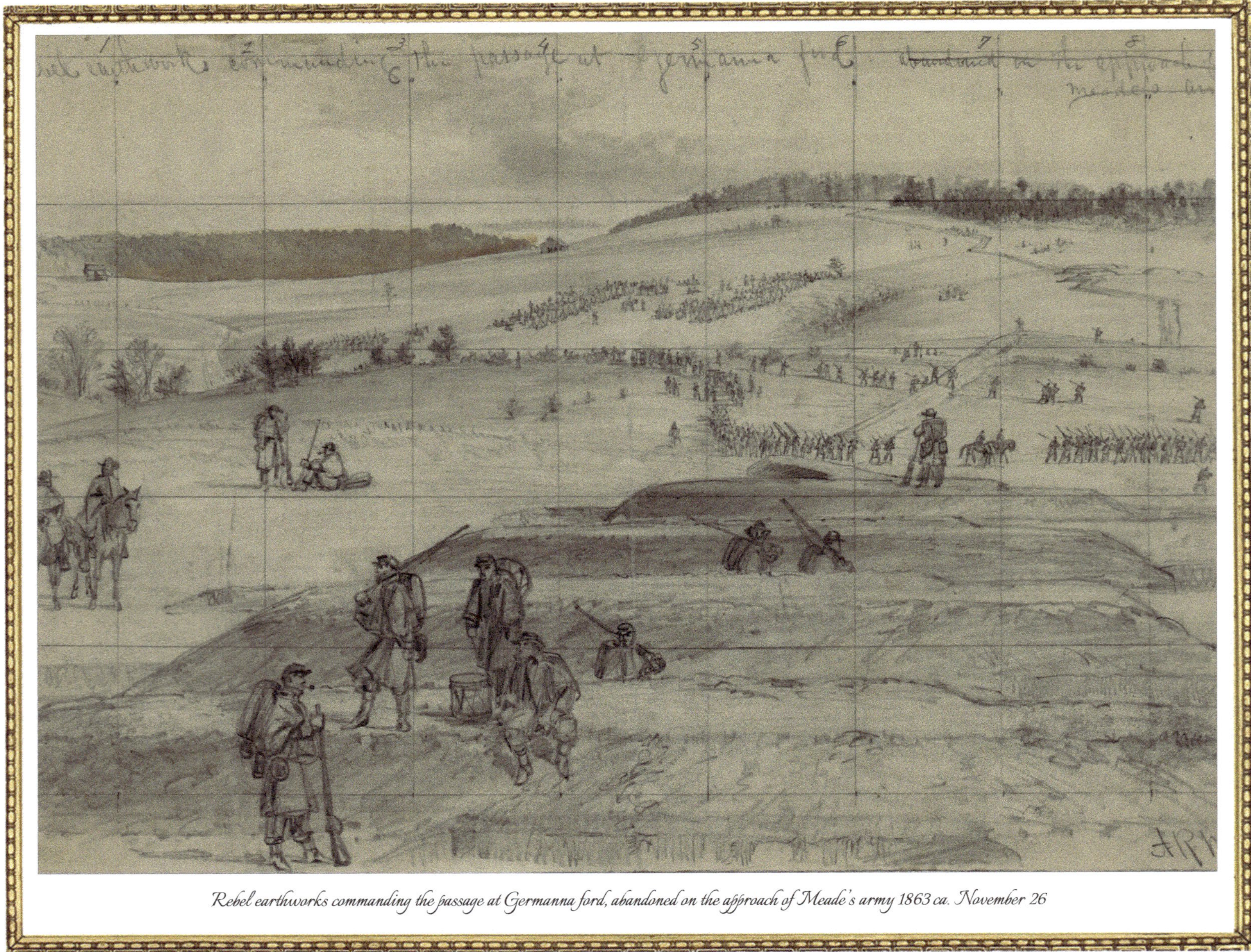

Rebel earthworks commanding the passage at Germanna ford, abandoned on the approach of Meade's army 1863 ca. November 26

Scene at the late reconnaissance at Morton Ford at night, 1864 February 6-7

Lt. Porter tries spherical case, and shell 1864 March

Freedmans village Greene Heights Arlington, VA. 1864 April

Union artillery at Petersburg 1864

Headquarters of Gen.l Warren at Col. Avery's house near Petersburg 1864

Genl. Wadsworths division in action in the Wilderness, near the spot where the General was killed 1864 May 5-7

Grants Great Campaign the New York 14th Heavy Artilery crossing Chesterfield Bridge, on the North Anna, under a heavy artillery fire 1864 ca. May 31

2nd Corps, Batteries in position on the bank of the North Anna. 2nd Maine Battery, 1864 May

Death of Gen. Polk Pine Mountain, Kennesaw 1864 June 14

Genl Ludlow 1864

Ponton Bridge on the Appomattox below Petersburg--Point of Rocks, Butlers headquarters 1864 June-July

Sharpshooters 18th Corps 1864 July

Battery of mortars and light twelves. Lt. Jackson. 1st Connecticut heavy Arty . 18th Corps 1864 ca July

Siege of Petersburg 1864 July

General Warren fortifying his lines on the Weldon road 1864 September

Genl. Stevensons Headqurters, Harpers Ferry 1864 December

Spare cartridges 1864

African American soldiers mustered out at Little Rock, Arkansas 1865

The Freedmen's Bureau 1865

Richmond ladies going to receive government rations 1865

Sheridans army following Early up the Valley of the Shenandoah between 1864 August and 1865 March

The 24th Corps charging a fort to the left 1865 April 2

Richmond Firemen pushing down the remains of the burnt dwellings Capital Squar 1865 ca. April

Libby again Rebel soldiers waiting for accommodations in that Hotel 1865 April

The casemate, Fortress Monroe, Jeff Davis in prison 1865

A guerilla A deserter, no data insert

A bugler, no data insert

ACW BOOKS ALREADY PUBLISHED FROM SOLDIERSHOP

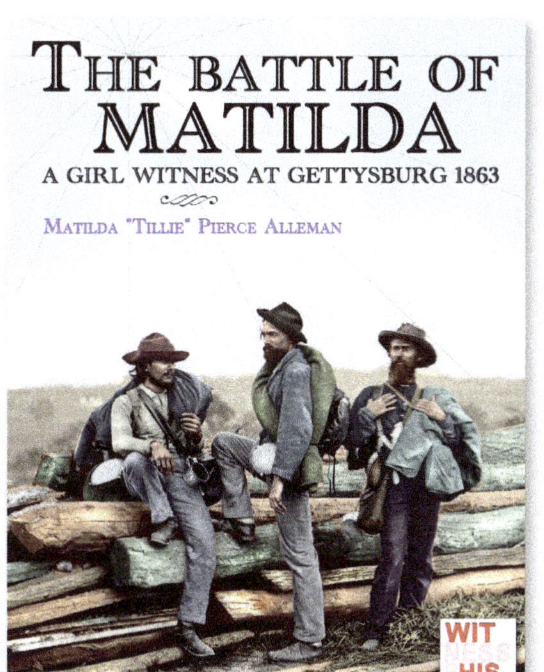

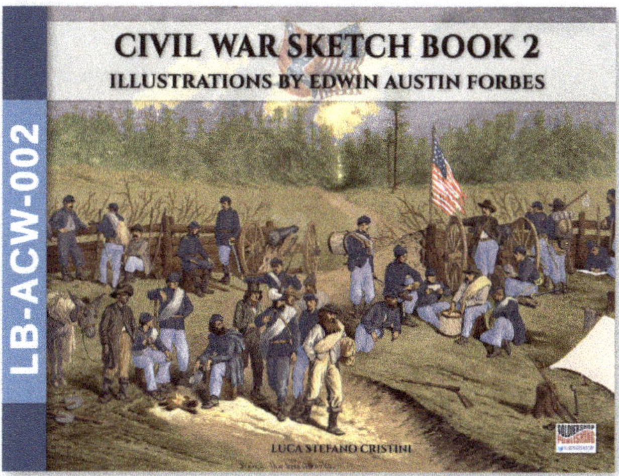

SOLDIERSHOP
PUBLISHING

CRI ED
STI ITO
NI RE

www.ingramcontent.com/pod-product-compliance
Lightning Source LLC
LaVergne TN
LVHW071526180726
843512LV00014B/1170